Pushing Through the Pain

to Pursue Your Purpose

June,
Its Time
To Push
Through!

Vanessa

Vanessa A. Fleeton

Unless otherwise noted, all Scripture quotations are from
the NIV Study Bible. 10th Anniversary Edition New
International Version Zondervan Publishing House Grand
Rapids, Michigan 49530 USA copyright ©1985, 1995, 2002

Editing, Layout and Cover Design: Karen Bowlding
Editing: Nakeia Daniels, The Writer's Fellowship Group
Cover Photography: The Captured Life Photography

Library of Congress Control Number: 2013913882
ISBN: 978-0-615-87784-6

Printed in the United States of America 2014

Dedication

To my heavenly Father who trusted me with this awesome task of sharing my pain for His purpose. If I had a thousand tongues, I couldn't thank you enough. You wiped every tear from my eyes and held me in Your arms when I felt lonely or scared. You've kept me through each trial and have allowed me to shine like pure gold. I hope I've made You proud.

To all God's children who feel unworthy of love; were born into an imperfect situation; feel that life is not full of multiple chances; believe that God will not forgive their particular sins; are in need of a self-love boost; need encouragement to pursue their purpose; or feel the emptiness of the lack of a parent's love, I pray that you will allow God to reign in your life and cover you in His love.

I pray that He will bless the work of my hands by using this book to forever change your life.

Acknowledgments

To my family and friends who have loved and supported me…I thank you from the bottom of my heart.

To all of my spiritual mothers and sisters in Christ…I so appreciate your encouragement, prayers, guidance and friendship throughout the years.

To my former and current church leaders, members, and ministry workers…you have sown into my life and helped me become the Christian woman I am today.

To those who poured into my vision either by working with me on this project or by helping me realize my purpose and the need to pursue it…I can't express how grateful I am for your efforts and support.

Introduction

Pushing Through the Pain to Pursue Your Purpose was written to inspire and motivate women and men of all ages to deal with and overcome past hurts so they can be free to walk in their pre-destined purpose.

This book will hopefully prompt readers to allow God to fill their void, repair all wounds of abandonment, heartaches and rejection, and clothe them with His love and acceptance.

The author encourages readers to get up, dust themselves off and begin a new chapter in their lives. You do have another chance at life. You can live a life without shame, guilt or anger and focus on the amazing destiny ahead.

Table of Contents

Dedication
Acknowledgments
Introduction

Part 1: Pushing Through the Pain

Part 2: To Pursue Your Purpose

Biography

Part 1

Pushing Through the Pain

1

Born into Rejection

Delivered on a bitter, cold evening in January, I was born into this world against all odds. I was a statistic before I could fathom what that meant. Based on the script the world had given me, I was on track to become an uneducated teenage mother on welfare. God had greater plans.

Jeremiah 29:11 says, *For I know the plans I have for you, declares the Lord, plans to prosper you, not to harm you, plans to give you hope and a future.*

A college student at the time of my birth, my father was only a few years older than my mother. Their relationship dissolved before I was born. He wasn't prepared. He and his parents were focused on his college goals, and didn't want my mother to give birth to me.

I strongly believe that it was no coincidence that God blessed my father with a daughter just nine months after the death of his mother on April 4, 1968, which was the day Martin Luther King was assassinated. God has a way of creating life in the midst of death. My paternal grandmother never laid her eyes on me, but I was given her middle name, Ada. Further proof that life can come from death.

After my grandmother died, my father was emotionally imbalanced. He chose to see me as an obligation, not a blessing. During one of our conversations, my father mentioned that he turned to drugs and became emotionally imbalanced. After speaking to him, I realized that maybe I was better off without him. He couldn't take care of himself, and certainly couldn't raise a child. I don't remember much about my father in my younger years, only what I heard from family members. I wasn't the type of child who sat next to the window waiting for his arrival. Something inside of me knew that he wasn't around; that he wasn't coming to see me. It's better to be completely gone, than fluctuate in and out of a child's life.

My father allowed his situation to dictate his actions. The truth is that he was emotionally inaccessible for reasons I may never know, and checked out for most of my life. I was told that my father came to visit, but never helped raise me; he always came empty-handed. Once he tried to take me to his family reunion, but because he didn't provide for me, my mother didn't allow me to go. Instances like this made it so I didn't know any of my father's family.

My mother once told me that my father's brother said I looked like a white man's baby because of my pale skin and straight black hair. Years later, my complexion changed and I begin to resemble my father.

My mother dropped out of high school when she became pregnant with me. We lived in a house with my grandparents. My grandmother offered to help raise me, but my mother decided that she would do it alone. She dreaded the day that my father would come back into my life, especially after her hard work was complete and I was already grown. During those early years, I was told that my mother and I were close. To her credit, she did the best she could raising me with what she knew, which was limited at her young age.

2

Living in an Unhealthy Place

A t the age of three, my stepfather entered into our lives. Even though I am grateful that he financially provided for me, I still missed the intimacy that only a father could provide.

My mother later birthed three girls, and since I was the oldest, she expected more out of me. By then, I was a teenager trying to figure things out for myself. She said that I should help raise my sisters because she raised me. I could barely take care of myself, and could not help to raise anyone else. I was scolded for not bringing food home for my sisters when I worked at fast food restaurants. All of her attention was placed on my sisters. I wasn't trying to disobey her; I was simply too young to help raise three younger sisters. That is when I first realized I had no interest in raising children. I was focused on what teenagers should be focused on; preparing my life for the future.

My mother wasn't careful with the negative thoughts she implanted in our minds. Not only did this dysfunction affect our generation, it has spilled over to my nephew's generation. My fear is that her negativity may carry into our family's future.

Today, my sisters and I still aren't close. As the matriarch of our family, my mother has a huge influence on our relationships.

Thinking back over my childhood, I am not sure if our mother deliberately caused division between us as a way of punishing me for my strong-willed personality, or if she was just behaving in a way that was natural to her. As I grew I became the daughter who didn't allow our mother to easily control what I said and did.

No matter how hard I tried, I couldn't rationalize her mistreatment of me; the underlying way she handled me. I couldn't quite figure it out. My young mind wondered what I had done to justify her contempt.

As I aged and matured, our relationship grew more distant. Not only was my mother verbally abusive, but she became emotionally and physically abusive as well.

My mother was not affectionate. I believe her behavior added to my attention deficit and my constant yearning for affection. I can't recall many times when she held me or told me she was proud of me and loved me. I do remember one incident when we were talking in the kitchen. She threatened to physically hurt me. I told her that I would call the police if she touched me again. Those are the memories I have of my mother.

I know she has her own story to tell, and I'm sure her scars are deeper than they seem. I understand that now, but then, I was too young to grasp the pain she must have lived in. I was too busy trying to make sense of my own pain.

With little guidance or assistance at home, I still excelled in school. My mother used to say I was book smart, but not boy smart. Too bad they didn't teach about relationships in school. If it was presented in lesson form, I would have aced it. My mother chose not to come to school functions or meetings. She didn't check on my educational progress. She said her presence wasn't needed because I rarely got into trouble, except for a couple of fights. The fact was that I wanted and needed her support and encouragement. It hurt when she displayed a lack of concern for my achievements. I believed that my mother responded with little interest in my life because of my independence and strength.

At 16, I had my first job at a fast food restaurant. My mother got upset when I asked her to remove her name from my savings account. I was no longer solely dependent upon her. That became another issue in our relationship. I even saved money from my minimum wage job and bought my first car. I was ambitious and determined to achieve my goals.

Due to the many arguments and fights in our house, I stayed in my room and only came out when I had to. My mother often argued with me and my stepfather. When he tried to take up for me, she argued with him. She hit and beat me when she was angry with me or frustrated with her situation. She often displayed anger, frustration, and unhappiness with her life and the choices she had made. It was no secret that she was discontented with the way her life turned out. I'm not sure if she wasn't close to me because I looked like my father and I reminded her of him. I did know that as I aged I grew weary trying to figure out why my mother mistreated me. It was exhausting.

My mother fought my stepfather, and because he was a laid back, easy going guy, he allowed her to do what she wanted, and she took advantage of him. My sisters were young, so they didn't get much of her wrath until they were older.

In addition to her unaffectionate demeanor, my mother was also critical. She talked down to me and said hurtful things; crushing my self-esteem with every foul word. She even taunted me about my positive attributes. She said, "Oh you're doing well, but you'll fall." Other times, when I was trying to better myself she said, "You're selfish, only looking out for yourself."

I valued peace, even when I was a young girl. When I disconnected with the family, my mother tried to destroy my name, reputation and relationships with other family members by spreading lies about me. Needless to say we rarely had good times or happiness in the house.

I have allergies and one of my sisters has a heart condition. Neither of these ailments convinced my parents not to smoke in our house. I hated breathing in that poison. I disliked going to the store to get cigarettes for my mother, but of course she was my mother so I had to do what I was told, in spite of it being wrong. I couldn't wait to leave the house so that I could put a no smoking rule on my life, in my house and in my car.

As a result of my abusive mother, I became a critical person, who also argued a lot. In high school,

I was voted most argumentative. Even though I was smart, talkative, and participated in extracurricular activities, that was the label I was given.

My last name was not the same as the rest of my family, but that didn't bother me. What did trouble me was that I always felt torn between two worlds; my mother's side of the family with whom I didn't feel any connection and my father's side of the family whom I didn't know.

In spite of the turmoil I experienced, some of my childhood was normal and fun. I had my own room with a lovely canopy bed; I had a pint-sized oven that I used to bake tiny treats; I received nice Christmas gifts; my favorite game was monopoly, and sometimes I played it with my friends next door and we jumped double-dutch. Once I asked my mother for a doll that looked like me. She tried to fool me by telling me that they didn't sell those types of dolls. I later realized that it was hard to find so she just gave me what was readily available. Nonetheless, I enjoyed my doll.

Growing up, our only vacations were weekend trips to visit family in Georgia. I remember crying every time we had to leave. I was thankful I had food, shelter and clothes; the basic necessities of life, but a great deal was still missing in my life. There are times when I reflect upon the fact that my upbringing could have been better, but it also could have been worse.

Although I started raising myself at an early age, I was grateful for the lessons. A lot of what I learned about life was through trial and error. My stepfather attempted to give me a bike riding lesson. He gave me instructions, but things went wrong when he left me and went into the house. After hearing a loud noise, my parents ran outside to find that I had crashed into two large trashcans. I panicked and turned left and drove down the hill instead of hitting the brakes. If I kept going, I would have ended up in the street. How's that for a crash course in bike riding?

That same bike caused my mother to pull a lady's head through the window of a front door. She didn't play when it came to messing with her children. The woman's daughter pushed me off my bike and tried to take it. I was surprised that she reacted that way, but mama-bear had to protect her cub!

Some lessons I mastered, but some I didn't. For instance, I taught myself basic life skills such as managing finances, driving, maintaining a house and car, cleaning, laundry and cooking. To her credit, my mother did try to teach me how to cook, but I felt her motive was self-serving, and she wasn't long on patience. Needless to say, it didn't work. I was more interested in school and extracurricular activities such as cheerleading, military training, business clubs, and working to make my own money.

Despite my parent's lack of parenting skills, I was able to go on and become a two-time graduate from college, a federal government employee for over 25 years, and an owner of my first car at 18 and first house at 26. I know God made it all possible.

I later understood that maybe my parent's job was to get me here and God would do the rest. Genesis 1:27 says, "*So God created man in his own image, in the image of God He created Him, male and female, He created them.*" I believe that's true, regardless of how I came into this world or my circumstances. As challenging as it was, I am much stronger, resilient and self-reliant because of my upbringing.

As I read Bible stories about Jesus and Moses, I realized that they weren't born into perfect situations, but their purpose was made perfect by the power of God. He used them to forever change the world.

It has been said that when a father leaves, he takes a part of his daughter's soul with him. The remaining part of my soul yearned for my mother's love. It didn't make sense at the time, but I know now that God makes no mistakes; there are no accidents in Christ. I couldn't change my parents, but I could change my perception. I no longer question God. He chose my parents, and He lets me know that He's got my back, every step of the way. Psalm 27:10 says, "*Though my father and mother forsake me, the Lord will receive me.*"

I asked God why my family was so distant. I remember my mother often got mad at me for talking to my father. I once told her that I should be mad, she chose him, not me. Well, that statement didn't go over too well.

Exodus 20:12 says, "*Honor your father and your mother, so that you may live long in the land the Lord your God is giving you.*" I forgave both of my parents, and still try to honor them the best way I know how. As painful as it is sometimes, I have to love my family from a distance until everyone can get on one accord. I'm in a good place right now, and I don't want to undue years of progress.

Despite my numerous requests, my family chose not to seek counsel, so it's hard for us to get to a healthy place; a place of respectable communication, unconditional love and forgiveness. I invited my mother to a counseling session years ago. She attended one session, and didn't return.

In my adults years, my father and I became closer. My mother expressed her disappointment, as she had many times over the years. She constantly reminded me that my father didn't want me. All these years later, those words still ring in my ears. I felt it was inappropriate to say such things to a child, no matter how you feel about her father. I knew that he could not give back the lost years, but because I wanted to have a relationship with him, I gave him many chances to make up for lost time.

Each time he failed me. I didn't trust that he would show up or help me the few times I needed him. I felt like he should have at least make an attempt to be the father I needed, especially since I was his only child.

It appeared that there were some things that he was not ready to give or capable of giving. I once asked my father to drive me to New Jersey to see a holistic doctor. I noticed a pattern of senseless arguments that arbitrarily sprung up between us, so I decided to let him be. I wanted our trip to be peaceful, not uncomfortable. We are estranged because of the argument we had over the trip.

I didn't have a close relationship with either of my grandfathers, both are deceased. My maternal grandfather, for whatever reason, didn't reach out to form a close relationship with me. My paternal grandfather cried every time he saw me, which wasn't often. He promised me the house that he and my grandmother shared, but on his terms. I had to agree to allow my father to stay there. Needless to say, I didn't agree, and the house was lost. A man took advantage of my grandfather while in his drinking condition. My grandfather allowed the man to use the house as collateral.

It's strange, but years later, the relationship with my father was strained over another house situation. I co-signed for my father and stepmother's house. Our relationship ended up being divided, further damaging my anticipated father-daughter bond. My mother was upset when she heard what I had done for them because I didn't co-sign for an apartment for her and my sisters.

What a whirlwind that turned out to be. It seemed no matter how hard I tried, I couldn't win for losing. I couldn't please anyone. When I tried, it backfired. In retrospect, I shouldn't have co-signed for anyone's house or apartment. As I matured, I realized that *no* is not a bad word. I know now that *no* has the potential to save relationships, not destroy them. When I bought my first house it was difficult because my name was on the mortgage of another house. When I presented the situation to my father, he was cold. We ended up in court. Years later, my name was finally removed from the mortgage.

I've had many losses in my young life. I had to push through the pain while remaining focused. I was devastated when my only Aunt tragically died. One day she was alive, and the next day she fell and broke her neck. Then there was the relocation of my only grandmother. I've always been close to my grandmother, which caused yet another rift between my mother and me. My grandmother signed me up at a karate school. After my first tournament, and right before I could get my next belt, my mother took me out. That was the only thing in life I didn't finish. My grandmother and aunt were my biggest supporters.

My grandmother left Maryland and returned to Georgia when I was a teenager, and that left another void. Having my grandmother's support and attention meant so much to me. I was in tears when she left because I was raised with her in my life, and couldn't imagine only seeing her once a year, as I do now.

One of the reasons I believe I survived my dysfunctional upbringing was because I was baptized and joined a church when I was 12 years old. I sang in the choir and attended all the church programs I could. God knew exactly what I would go through, and that I would make it in the end. He touched my heart as a young girl. I am forever grateful that He did.

Regardless of my past, I am becoming the woman God called me to be because I've allowed Him to fulfill the void in my soul. In spite of the issues during my childhood and the disappointments in my life, I survived. I am sane, whole and healed.

Recently, I was a vendor at a church event where the headlining gospel group, my old high school mates, honored their ill mother during a special Anniversary service. Surprised, I looked up from my table and my mother was standing there. I hadn't seen or talked to her in years. I could tell she had taken ill and wasn't herself, which really hurt me because I was used to seeing her healthy and strong.

It was a divine intervention. I knew that God set us up. My mother sat and talked with me and asked me why I was selling items. She stated that she didn't have any money, even though she looked at me through designer frames and said that she would buy a CD from the gospel group moments before.

It would have been nice to have her support, but I didn't get that. I resolved that even though our relationship is estranged, she is my mother. What did I do? I gave her whatever she wanted…no charge.

As I sat there watching and listening to the group's dedication to their mother, I couldn't hold back my tears. I went to the front door to get some air and then to the bathroom. My mother walked in, and all I wanted to do was hug her and tell her that I loved her, but I decided to keep it together instead. I was so accustomed to getting hurt by her. I figured that if I had no expectations I would be able to guard myself against hurt on top of hurt.

As she left, she offered to help me. I told her that she didn't have to. She left, and that was it. I tried to dry my tears. Our relationship is what it is. I said a prayer for my mother. I went home and continued on with my life; so that I wouldn't break all the way down.

3

The Spiral

Upon entering high school, I found myself quickly spiraling downward. No longer the bright-eyed middle-school girl, I didn't know how to handle my emotions or situations that I had to deal with. I started to make poor decisions; searching for love and attention in the arms of many guys. I needed to be needed and I wanted to be wanted. I longed to be held and feel safe.

There was a deficit in too many areas of my life. I was attention starved, and did anything to get it. I left the teachings of God, and began a life of promiscuity. It was obvious to anyone who cared enough to see me that my low self-esteem and the missing love from my parents had a negative effect on me.

Three relationships forever changed my life. When I was a freshman in high school I dated a guy who was a senior at another school. He was a typical guy, nothing out of the ordinary or extraordinary. Our barely one-year relationship was nothing to write home about. He gave me tennis shoes as a gift. I was attracted to the attention I received from him and the connection to his family; I had none with mine. My mother actually allowed me to spend a day with him and his family at the beach. During my first visit to the beach, I was stung by a jellyfish. I started skipping school to be with him at his house. I was young and made bad decisions. I gave him my virginity. I can't say that it was fireworks. At 14, I wasn't emotionally or physically ready.

The relationship ended when I found out that he was seeing a senior at my school. She approached me and we ended up fighting in the halls and again outside later that same day; over a guy who didn't care about either of us. It's amazing what sin and pride will push you to do. I still have the bite mark on my inner thigh to prove it. To top it all off, I was suspended from school.

At that time my self-esteem was low. I didn't feel attractive because my hair began to fall out due to a bad relaxer. I didn't maintain my honor roll status. I was bleeding on the inside, but happy to get some attention.

I found myself yet again looking for love in the arms of a man. It was during my senior year of high school when I started dating a young man in a gospel group. He was a few years older, and I was crazy about him. We spent a lot of time together. I attended his gospel programs and he my cheerleading events. He even had my initials engraved into the back of his hair. By then I was head-over-heels in love. We got so close that I went to the doctor to get birth control pills. I was told by the doctor that I had to be careful when taking the pill because I had fibrocystic breasts; a condition I realized after my boyfriend found a lump in my breast. Soon after, I stopped taking the pills because of the health scare and the history of breast cancer in my family. Later in life, I realized that if I was going to choose not to take the pill, I needed to demand that a guy used some form of protection during every sexual interaction.

My older boyfriend gave me a pre-engagement ring. Unfortunately, during a weekend spent out of town at his relatives' home, I couldn't find the ring the next morning. He had no idea what happened to it.

We both *knew* God, but the relationship did not resemble a Christian relationship. He introduced me to wine coolers, pornography, and other sexual acts that I was too young to handle. Normally, those were things I would not do because I knew better, but because I wanted to be with him, I slowly drifted away from God, from my church and its teachings.

One day, I woke up and he was gone. I was quite confused because we never argued. Even though my mother also dated someone in the group, no one told me where he was or what went wrong. After doing things that I knew I shouldn't have done to be with him, he still left. That was my first heartbreak. I was devastated. With all of the unanswered questions and grief, I somehow was able to muster through my feelings enough to begin my freshman year in college and my first year as a federal government employee.

Two years later he came back into my life. I found out that he was dating another woman and had a child with her. I wondered if I was too naive for him, and he chose someone more experienced. Although I still had strong feelings for him, I did not take him back. I'm thankful to God that I had the strength to resist, especially since he had more baggage than what he left with. At 20, I didn't want to be anyone's stepmother.

I didn't understand why he left. A few years ago, he tried to come back a third time. He contacted me through a social media website. We exchanged communication a few times, but once I prayed about it, I later understood that God removed him from my life for a reason. Later on, both of us cleared the air. He told me that we argued on the day he left because I didn't want him to go out. I couldn't deny it. My abandonment issues were serious. I ended all communication with him, and honored God's whisper to me to leave the past behind me.

I met another young man who was a senior in high school when I was a sophomore in college. He was from a two-parent household and was making plans to attend college. After dating for a year, I became pregnant. We didn't share that information with anyone, except two of our closest friends. After discussing it, we decided to terminate the pregnancy. That was the first of three terminations. As awful as that sounds, imagine my brokenness and emptiness. I was hollowed glass by that time. Young, in pain, and with little hope, I felt that it was the best decision we could make at the time. I believed there were no other options that were best. For years I felt horrible, and wondered how our relationship would have turned out if we stayed together and had the baby; wondered what kind of child we would have had. Not a day goes by that I don't think about those choices.

I remember my close friend frowning on me as I made that difficult decision. She was the girlfriend of my boyfriend's best friend. They all were a couple of years younger than me. Once she came across her own life's challenges, she was able to relate to my situation. She didn't understand until she went through it herself. We talked about her situation and moved on. I decided not to return the judgmental treatment she so graciously bestowed upon me. It isn't in my nature to purposefully mistreat anyone.

At the age of 21, my mother put me out of her house. My boyfriend was away at college and I felt alone. My uncle was kind enough to give me his bedroom. I continued to spiral out of control and my life was empty.

I connected with a guy who had previously dated my friend. She was very close with my former boyfriend...a little too close. Subconsciously, I might have wanted to get back at her. To some extent, I lived with her ex-boyfriend and his family. Shortly afterwards, I again found myself pregnant. I only shared my secret with my friend. I was on the floor and up against the wall, in tears as I spilled my guts to her over the phone. After I confided in her, my so-called friend told my now former boyfriend all of my secrets. On the day of the procedure I was locked in my Uncle's house. I was so desperate that I climbed over the balcony and went to the clinic. I later discovered that he cheated on me, and I ended the relationship.

I felt ashamed, regretful, sinful, empty, unloved, alone, and fearful as a result of the relationships and the consequences of them. Those decisions haunted me in a serious way for over twenty years, and still affects me to this day. For years, when I saw babies, I bawled. I constantly prayed for forgiveness. God told me that he forgave me every time I asked him. When God forgives, you are truly forgiven. I am grateful to God for His mercy.

By the time I terminated my last pregnancy I was living on my own. After sticking to my promise of only living with my Uncle for three months, I moved into my first apartment. When I first moved in, I accidently locked myself in the bathroom. I yelled out the window and asked a complete stranger to help me. I threw my keys out the window and prayed that he wouldn't harm or steal from me. I was in the *hood*, not suburbia. A stranger arrived with my keys and opened the door for me. I was so grateful for his help and God's protection. I was released and unharmed.

The pain I suffered in my childhood caused a lot of damage. I wish someone would have shown me what real love looked and felt like. I wish I had an opportunity to emotionally heal before coming into contact with my boyfriends.

Back then, I displayed textbook abandonment behavior. I ran away from pain and sought love from all the wrong places for comfort. I dated a lot, and I can't seem to remember why some relationships ended. I wish I had known that I should have entered into relationships with the expectation of being treated as a queen; as a woman of value and great worth.

Although I was emotionally damaged by the relationships I had been in, I experienced physical abuse only once by the hands of a man; he was an alcoholic. That was enough for me. While arguing in his face, he pushed me down. I raised a knife, and nipped his back. Fortunately, his roommate grabbed my hand and kept me from stabbing him. Needless to say, we didn't last long after that incident.

I wish I had stayed close to God because He was the only one who could have filled my void. I wish I was told that I was special and beautiful. I wish I knew then that God loved me, created me fearfully and wonderfully, and that He loved me more than words could express, even after I left Him and sinned against Him. Little did I know at the time, but God was with me all along. I just had to let Him back into my life.

4

Married, Yet Still Incomplete

January 2000 started with a traumatic experience. A fire incinerated my kitchen. I had to go to the laundry mat to wash clothes. I was looking and smelling a hot mess. While at the laundry mat, a guy asked if he could offer his friendship. I wasn't prepared for what came afterward.

We quickly developed a close relationship. He picked me up and rode me through the snow. He was a perfect gentleman; he opened doors, cooked for me, and showed me lots of attention. I was impressed by him. He was the first man who treated me like I was worth the wait.

When I decided to accept his hand in marriage, I was at a transitional period in my life. At the time, I felt that I had achieved everything I wanted. The only thing missing was a husband. Knowing we weren't ready, my emotional emptiness and unresolved pain sparked the *need* to marry him. We knew each other for less than a year. I had made yet another decision out of my brokenness. My background did not prepare me for marriage. That was re-emphasized when his mother asked me if my parents were married.

We went through a few counseling sessions, and I saw the red flags. I expressed my concerns to the pastor we were seeing. He said that the devil may not want us to get married. We later met with another pastor, the one who eventually married us. He was my great-aunt's husband, the same pastor that married my mother. All he wanted to know was if we loved each other.

As we prepared for our wedding, many things went wrong. I was over an hour late to the ceremony, and was quite nervous while walking down the aisle.

As we exchanged our vows, I barely looked at him. His family threatened not to show up, but later changed their minds. My immediate family didn't show up, and once again, they missed another important event in my life.

We consummated our marriage for the first time on our honeymoon in the Poconos. While this is a romantic place frequented by many honeymooners, I soon realized that something was missing with my new husband; friendship and intimacy.

Even though we were married, I still wasn't free to enjoy closeness because I feared pregnancy. I didn't want to bring a child into the world while dealing with issues I was still trying to conquer within myself and the marriage. I was afraid that my husband would leave me; just like my father. He had no idea that he married an abandoned little girl who was not ready emotionally, physically, mentally and spiritually to be a wife. I even told him during an argument that he would leave me just like my father did. Obviously I was still battling abandonment issues.

One day my husband told me about a church he heard about. It was the same pastor I recently saw on the television. I took it as a sign, and joined that church. On that particular day, my husband was not in attendance. For a short while we attended church together. After we began to have marital problems, he stopped attending.

Our relationship began to suffer. So many things happened between us as we went back and forth in the relationship. We had no idea how to separate ourselves for a successful reconciliation. We were good people, but not good for each other. It became apparent that we made a mistake. At that time, I stopped praying for my marriage and begin to pray for his salvation. His relationship with God was more important. Years later, I was told that he had returned to church and was doing well.

He knew God because he grew up in the Catholic Church, but I didn't want our trials to push him away from church or religion. I tried to make it work by attending classes and counseling sessions. He also attended the classes, but did not complete them.

I later realized that I failed to discern between a future best friend and a future husband. All friends don't make good husbands. I'm sure lots of friendships were destroyed because people moved on emotion, and didn't take the time to compartmentalize people. I was not prepared to enter into a lifetime relationship.

A well-known pastor gave me a revelation over the pulpit at a huge conference out of town. He said, "You're married to someone and you're complete opposites. Get a divorce and get it now because he'll prolong it." A representative came to me and told me that the pastor wanted to talk me. At the end of the talk, the pastor asked me if I would pursue my purpose if I stayed in the marriage. I told him that I believed I would forfeit my purpose. You can only imagine what my husband and others thought when I shared that revelation. I didn't care, but after that experience, my answer was final.

I started being honest with myself about where I was emotionally, and how I arrived there. As I became more comfortable with being human and not being perfect, the shameful feelings I carried subsided. I was finally learning to accept God's love, forgiveness and comfort in my life.

In June 2005, just five short years after getting married, I found myself once again all alone in court, all because my ex-husband didn't agree with our divorce. To his defense, while we were divorcing, my ex-husband visited me in the hospital when I had surgery. That was my first time spending a night in a hospital, so I needed the company.

I realized that I may have married my husband to stop the downward spiral that I was in. I no longer had to trade myself for a temporary fix or the imitation of love. I was not close to being healthy as it pertained to relationships. I knew that I would commit to sleeping with one man, but little did I know, our marriage would never survive even if the spiral had stopped. Still, the decision to divorce was difficult.

5

A Divorced Christian

The next journey of my life was challenging because I was a divorced Christian trying to please God. Malachi 2:16a says, "*I hate divorce, says the Lord, the God of Israel...*"

The Bible does not say that God hates me or anyone else that is divorced. It actually says that He hates divorce; the act itself. I truly believe God is forgiving; a God of multiple chances. Some people, including Christians, will try to make you feel bad because you're a divorcee.

A close friend verbalized negative statements to me about my decision, but I had to do what was best for me and what I felt was best for our situation.

Some people judged your sins based on limited knowledge. They are really hard on the sins in which they don't commit, not realizing that we *all* fall short of the glory of God.

Yes, we know that God hates divorce, but God hates all sin. There are different situations that we all might find ourselves in, but Jesus Christ died for all of our sins. The truth is we are forgiven. 1 John 1:9 states, *"If we confess our sins, he is faithful and just and will forgive us our sins and purify us from all unrighteousness."*

Despite the fact that my marriage did not work out, I believe God used the marriage to teach me some lessons and to make me into the woman I am today. In my past, I created unhealthy spiritual ties with various men. I had to ask God to break every bond and make me into a new creature.

I am now in an unfamiliar state because I've never waited on God for a mate. I've been practicing celibacy for over 10 years, as my ex-husband is the last person I was intimate with. I'm learning how to maintain sex-less friendships, date, and court as a Christian.

I have not dated a lot as a Christian. I was tested a couple of years ago. During a Thanksgiving dinner at a church member's relatives' house, I met a man. From the beginning he was told of my boundaries, but I guess he thought he could change my mind. He attended church with me on New Year's Eve; I was not going to miss out on bringing in the New Year outside of church, new man or not. He also served with me at a local homeless shelter.

As time went on, I began to lower my standards. We spent time at my house and I visited him once at his. We hung out and talked on the phone until the wee hours of the morning. The act of sex entered the conversation a few times. He had the nerve to debate with me about whether Adam and Eve were married or not. He went too far. I should have delivered my exit speech right then.

One evening, we spent too much time on the couch, supposedly watching television, and we started to hug and kiss. By then, I had been single for over five years, and I knew that was a *no, no.* Another particular night, we got close to the bedroom, and that was my cue to put on the brakes. What was I doing?

1 Corinthians 10:13 says, *"No temptation has overtaken you except what is common to mankind. And God is faithful; he will not let you be tempted beyond what you can bear. But when you are tempted, he will also provide a way out so that you can endure it."* I was satisfying my flesh, while my spirit suffered.

I wondered how my ministry to women would be affected if I gave in. I wouldn't be able to tell them to wait for their husband. How would my testimony change? How would that situation affect the anointing that I knew was on my life? How could I continue to walk around with my head held high and experience the freedom I have today? How could I show up without my purity ring? These were the questions that flooded my mind.

Everyone who knows me is familiar with the meaning and inscription on the ring on my right ring finger, "I will wait for my true love." I'm so proud of my sexual status that I could yell it at the top of the Washington Monument. We ended our dating escapade in January, days before my birthday. Whew! I had passed the test. That was a close one.

Once again, God completely removed him from my life; he just disappeared. God really knows how to do it. James 4:7 says, "*Submit yourselves, then, to God. Resist the devil, and he will flee from you.*" He attempted to come back months later, but I had gained strength from resisting temptation the first time. There was nothing left for us to talk about.

Please understand that I am still careful when interacting with men. I no longer put myself in compromising positions. I know my boundaries and the lifestyle I desire to live. If you make a conscience decision about how you are going to live your life, you need guidelines to protect yourself. It's not easy being single, but as long as I focus on my promise, I'll make it, and if you're a single believer, so can you!

I have a list of twenty qualities I want in a husband, but this is only a request. I know God has the final say, but there's no harm in asking. I'm determined to wait because God knows what's best for me and he also knows the right time.

Our time is not God's time. My prayer is that God prepares me while I'm waiting, and that I remain open to what He has for me. I choose every day to wait on God. Proverbs 31:10 says, "*A wife of noble character who can find? She is worth far more than rubies.*" I'm determined to wait on my prince. And, I am encouraged…he will find me.

In a scene from a play, the lead actor said that in your twenties you have pages and pages of what you want in a man. By the time you reach your forties and fifties, it's just five words, "Lord let him be breathing!" I've narrowed my list to three: (1) He must love and worship the Lord God, (2) He must love and respect himself, and (3) He must love and honor me. It won't hurt to get a full background check that includes his mental, financial, health, spiritual condition and marital status! And of course, we'll have to go through the process of friendship, courting, and counseling *before* marriage.

I'm now comfortable saying what I want and don't want in my life. I want a companion, but I'm content in my current situation. I'm not trying to beat the biological clock. I love babies, even babysat for a church member and later became an Auntie, which is enough for me.

My life resembles nothing like it did before. I know who I am and whose I am. I remember clearly the day God called me away from night clubs. I was sitting in a booth in a club I frequented, and my fun was slowly diminishing. I knew that it was to be my last time there.

I try to carry myself as a real lady. I believe there's a difference between a woman and a lady. I dress conservative, but I like to keep it *sassy*. Proverbs 31:30 says, *"Charm is deceptive and beauty is fleeting, but a woman who fears the Lord is to be praised."* I command, not demand respect. I will admit, I do get a lot of flirtatious requests, but once they see evidence of my commitment to live a life without fornication or see that I don't *play house*, the communication usually stops. I think God has put a shield of protection around me because I don't get a lot of *holler-backs* like I did in the world. That's fine with me because I no longer want, nor do I crave all the attention; I want the right attention.

If you're single waiting for your mate, a job, or anything from God, remember that Ecclesiastes 3:1 says, "*There is a time for everything, and a season for every activity under the heavens.*"

6

The Journey Back to My First Love

My journey back to God, my first love; back to where joy began, started while I was still married. After my ex-husband left our home church, I continued to serve on the intercessory prayer team and homeless ministry. As I continued to attend church, my healing accelerated.

One event in particular led me to the decision to allow God to use me. There was a tell-all session for teenage girls, and I stood before an entire audience and shared my past shames and secrets. That was my journey to travel, even if that meant I had to be exposed.

Years later, I was chosen to go on a mission trip with my church to South Africa. That trip forever changed my life. The people there had very little, but they praised God as if they were living in mansions; without a care in the world. I was given an African name that meant prayer. We received so much love, I could barely hold in my emotions. I cried almost every day.

Shortly before I was chosen, I had a dream that I was in a foreign land at a school. After I had finally made it there, I heard my assignment. I was to be involved with a school; that was where God wanted me. I started crying again.

I was a different person when I returned home. I hated waste and was more appreciative of what I had. After my wonderful experience and returning home, my family's comments put a damper on things. They wondered why I traveled so far to help people when there were people here in the States and in our family who needed help. Their comments didn't matter. I was used to doing what was right, not what was right for others.

A couple of years later, I had another dream. I was floating in water and I had on a white garment. One of the leaders at the church was above my head. Shortly after, the same leader stood in the pulpit and talked about getting baptized. The invitation for baptism wasn't given every Sunday so I knew what I had to do next. When they brought me up from the water, I was frantic because it was freezing cold, and I thought they were trying to drown me. I didn't know how to swim. Thankfully, that was not the case, and all was well when I came out of the water.

My next journey was at another church. After 12 years, it was time to leave my current church. It wasn't an easy choice to make, but I knew it was time to go. For months I didn't attend church. I went through a season where I just couldn't get it together. I thank God that he didn't leave me during my low times. On Mother's Day of 2013, I visited my current church. I joined on Father's Day of 2013. In retrospect, maybe those dates are symbolic for reuniting with my spiritual parent...God.

Every week, I received new confirmations on my purpose. On Easter Sunday 2013, my Pastor talked about the wisdom in your wounds. He related it to the wounds Jesus suffered when he was crucified. He said it's good to encourage people and tell them about the love of Jesus, but some people need to know your story and how you got those wounds. He further explained that everyone can't handle your wound stories, but every now and then, people need to know your sins and how you overcame. I heard it said that you can't heal wounds when they're covered up. This is one reason why I wrote this book.

As I returned to my first love, my self-esteem issues were no more. I remember growing up being self-conscious about my hair. My hair first came out when my mother played kitchen beautician. I didn't have long hair and was often called names. After I grew up and realized who I was in Christ, and after my visit to the motherland, I let go of hair perms and locked my hair.

It's been over seven years, and I love my crinkly, natural locks. I've already cut two inches from the back, so I'm no longer concerned with the length, but only the healthiness of my hair. I love myself and how I look. Only God could take me to a place where I would begin to see myself as He sees me.

I heard a story on the radio about a lady who wanted to impress her husband. She felt insecure about her measurements because her breasts were not proportionate to the rest of her body. Her insecurities made her feel like her husband was focusing on other women's breasts that were much larger. She told her husband she was getting a knot removed and had breast enlargement surgery instead. After the surgery, she recognized that her nipples were not even. When her husband realized what she'd done, he said, "Your breasts were fine, you didn't need surgery." She called her doctor to see what could be done and he said, "You get what you pay for." She wrote a letter to the radio station because she didn't know what to do; leave them as is or go under the knife once again. I say, "Just be happy with yourself."

There was even a point in my life where I realized that somewhere along the way, I became a perfectionist. It could have been my attempt to make my parents love me more or have them be proud of me. I've now realized that perfection doesn't exist, but excellence does. And, the only one I must please is God. If I'm good enough for Him, I'm good enough.

7

Committed to My Purpose

Romans 8:28 says, "*All things work together for the good of those who love the Lord and are called according to his purpose.*" I felt like the enemy was trying to terminate my purpose. God started preparing me for my purpose when He allowed my secrets to be uncovered. He allowed someone close to me to air all my dirty laundry to my future in-laws. I'm so glad that I was honest about my past mistakes and promiscuity. My ex-husband wasn't caught off guard.

When he heard the news, he immediately shared it with me. He was cool about it, and I can credit that to the fact that I was honest with him and even suggested that we get an HIV test. He wouldn't reveal to me who the person was that betrayed me. I believe it was a woman who I thought at the time was my best friend. She tried to convince me that it wasn't her, but she's the only one that had contact with my new in-laws and knew my business in detail.

Needless to say, she dropped out of the wedding party and didn't attend the wedding. Our friendship quickly ended. He remained friends with her and her husband, which made me a little uncomfortable, but I tried to accept it.

As the years passed, God began to reveal my purpose, layer by layer. My purpose is to use my life's testimony to motivate others to push through their pain to pursue their life's purpose. What's your purpose? Take a moment and think about that. What are you on earth to do? Do you know? If not, ask God. He will reveal it to you. If you know, take a moment and write it down and place it somewhere safe. Never forget it. It's your roadmap for living.

At this point in my life I am not pressed to be in a relationship. It would be nice, but it's not my main concern. Being single and celibate plays an important part in my life and my commitment to my purpose because I'm free to focus on my life's work. I'm not wasting time wondering who or where Mr. Right is, and when he is going to show his face. I've never been so free in my life. I'm free from the emotional pain of speculating if he likes me or not, if I'm good enough or not or if he will run when I tell him the promise I made to God.

It took time, but I realize now that every man that comes into my life isn't a potential mate. He could be a business connection, it could be a witnessing opportunity; an opportunity for me to introduce them to God as my brother-in-Christ, or just to show me that male friends really exist. You have to keep things in perspective so that you can be honest with them and yourself. At this point, I'm successfully single, and will one day be successfully married. I know when I do meet my future-husband, he'll know and follow his purpose and he'll support me in pursuing mine.

I was blessed to have an experience with Cee Cee Michaela Floyd of Godz Girl Network. I connected with her after she attended a function at my former church. I was interested in learning more about her mission. I reached out and we discussed her ministry of helping young girls. Because I was passionate about making a difference in the lives of girls around the world, I felt that we both could benefit if we connected.

She mentioned to me that she had a documentary coming out, and because I had a testimony dealing with being a *second-chance* virgin, I travelled to Atlanta to participate in the documentary.

Following the video shoot, I attended one of her events in Atlanta, GA. At the end of the program, women were given purity rings, re-dedicated their body to God, and were restored; a born-again virgin.

That was the first time I was introduced to that type of event. My life was forever changed. It was truly a blessing to be around other women who valued their relationship with God and knew that no matter what happened in their past, God would reestablish them. I purchased a ring and wore it for a while. I made the promise to God to wait on my husband.

I bought another ring that has a cross inside of a heart and it is inscribed with *I'll wait for my true love.* The first time I ordered the ring, it was not delivered, but I was determined, so I reordered it. The significance of the ring is that my heart and spirit remains with God. When my husband comes along, my body will be united with him, and we'll both have a heart for God. You too can be restored, fulfilled and practice celibacy until your husband finds you (if you're a woman), or until you find your wife (if you're a man). As you make your decision, here's a few things to think about. There are several reasons for remaining celibate. By doing so you will:

- Honor God with your body.
- Live free from emotional, mental, and physical heartache.
- Reduce the years of breaking emotional and spiritual ties.
- Avoid temptation.

- Protect yourself from creating children out of wedlock.
- Protect yourself from sexually transmitted diseases.
- Be a walking, talking, living, breathing example for others that celibacy can be done.
- Give your future spouse the best gift ever… YOU!

Years later, I met Lindsey Marsh Warren of "Worth the Wait Revolution". I read a story about Mrs. Warren and her husband in the newspaper. I was so impressed that I started to follow her ministry. I attended a few of her functions and bought her first book. Well, as God would have it, my secret testimony is in her second book. Being chosen to be a part of that project let me know that it was time for me to share my story and secrets.

I presented a copy of Lindsey's book to my uncle. I didn't know what to expect, so I gave him a few days to think about it. I asked him what he thought, and he responded that I must be a strong person to make it through all of that.

As I move on and continue in this journey called life, I find myself utilizing the tools gathered over the years to deal with day to day situations.

I am dealing with a situation as I pen these pages. I was in the hospital waiting room, expecting my grandmother to come out after taking a brain test. The doctor confirmed that a small tumor was on her brain. Her best options were to use radiation to shrink the tumor or keep an eye on it due to her age. At the time she was eighty-six years old. When I left Georgia, I knew that upon my next visit she would be in a nursing home. I was equipped for what was ahead.

When I started this project, I didn't know much about writing a book. I knew a few authors, but didn't know where to start. I just knew that I had to fulfill a purpose that had been burning in my spirit for years. I knew my friends were tired of hearing me talk about this book. I kept it on my bucket list. I began to interview editors and ghost writers. I was finally sent to a woman by someone I met at a church event. I learned quite a bit during my first meeting.

My second consultation was just the opposite. After the meeting I was so frustrated that I sat in my car in front of a convenience store and cried. As I walked around the store shopping for my items, I ate, not one, but two candy bars with almonds. I don't drink, smoke or engage in sexual relations, so I had to find the next best legal Christian thing to do...chocolate.

She was referred to me by an author friend, and claimed that God told her to work with me. 1John 4:1 says, *"Dear friends, do not believe every spirit, but test the spirits to see whether they are from God, because many false prophets have gone out into the world."* I went home and prayed. When I tell you that you have to push through, I mean you *really* have to push through.

I was led to another editor that worked on my book for several months. My release date was delayed, and after careful consideration, I decided to finish the book with the last two editors that were referred to me by church members and friends.

Sometimes, an interruption in your purpose is God's divine delay. I'm so glad that I was patient and trusted God. Praise God, because of my desire to push through the pain, you have my completed project in your hands.

It took a lot of vulnerability, humility, openness, honesty and God's grace for me to write this book. If God can turn my struggle into a story it was all worth it. It took several years before I decided to write this book because I believed that I would be judged. I also waited for a ghost writer, and since I did not connect with one, I started to get frustrated. It was time to push again!

Through the wise advice from a friend, I prepared to write my book. I developed a plan and determined the reason and who the audience would be. I've always been a visionary. I visualize myself speaking to large audiences and selling books all over the world. Sometimes you just have to speak it into existence; see yourself walking in your purpose. It was lights, camera, and action after that!

I purchased a laptop. I was proud of myself for stepping up in technology and stepping out by writing. During this process, I had to let go of my flip-phone and buy a smart phone, which was inoperable for over a week because I dropped it in a public bathroom toilet. God worked a miracle on this past Christmas Eve and my phone was mostly repaired and working again.

By not upgrading for over two years, I saved over $1,000. I used the money to fund my purpose and now I can write my new phone off on my taxes; it worked out. I'm still getting more familiar with social networking, but I'm on my way. I wasn't going to let those minor details keep me from writing, and neither should you. With God, nothing is impossible.

I made a vow that by the end of 2013 my first book would be published. My author friends encouraged me. Once I saw they did it, I knew that I could too. I encourage you to allow me to be the author-friend that shows that you can do it too. I dare you to dream. I double-dog dare you to reach your destiny!

I heard this statement while watching one of my favorite movies, "If you want to know the function of a thing, ask the manufacturer." Well, God is our manufacturer. I had to pray to God and prepare myself while I waited for the answer. After several confirmations, I had to get going on my purpose. I'd hate to see my Heavenly Father and try to explain why I spent years on earth and didn't achieve my purpose.

I've been alone on this journey for most of my life. I recently was told that pioneers often have to travel alone, as they're unique people and often misunderstood. Jeremiah 1:5 says, *"Before I formed you in the womb, I knew you, before you were born, I set you apart; I appointed you as a prophet to the nations."* I've always been more of a loner, however, I can mingle with the best of them, and I've never met a stranger.

I am not saying that the road to end up where I am now was easy. I needed help on this journey. For almost a year, I dealt with a mild case of depression. The enemy knows when your blessing is around the corner or when you're close to fulfilling your purpose. I didn't want to attend church. It was hard to get out of bed before 11 o'clock in the morning. There was a time when I didn't enjoy the things I loved to do. I didn't go out like I used to. It was a terrible time.

Because I am not close to my immediate family, life can be difficult, especially during the holidays. I have to quickly catch myself and realize that it's only one day. I have the rest of my life to look forward to; for joy surely comes in the morning. Now that I know what events trigger certain emotions in me, I don't allow myself to get too far into depression, knowing that God always sends people my way to show me love.

Thank God, He reached down, touched me and gave me my joy back! I found myself looking for information and resources to help me get stronger. I attended spiritual counseling for six months to overcome some of the pain from my past. I was determined to go through. My spiritual counselor and I worked out many issues. After our sessions I felt better; but I still keep my therapist on speed-dial just in case. Proverbs 15:22 states, *"Plans fail for lack of counsel, but with many advisers they succeed."*

Your latter will be better than your former. I ask today that you believe in yourself because it's never too late. Things happen in life, but you have to be determined to be blessed, not broken. Focus more on what's right, not what's wrong. You may be dealing with physical pain as I have for over four years. That too, you can push past, just ask God to heal your body, focus on the mission and keep moving.

I'm a survivor and a champion. My mission is to encourage others that if they don't quit, eventually they'll come out on top. I want you to have a blessed life with a purposeful ending. Life is not perfect, but you can trade in your regrets for righteousness. You too can live a satisfied and saved life. I'm sure you've survived many trials, so I encourage you to allow God to turn it around.

The *V* in my first name no longer means Victim. I am Virtuous and Victorious!

The *A* in my middle name no longer means Abandoned. I am Anointed and Awesome!

The *F* in last name no longer means Fearful. I am Faithful and Fearless!

Now you create your own acronym!

Prayer for Purpose

"Father, I come to you today opening myself up to allow you to reveal my purpose on earth. I truly understand that our main purpose on earth is to glorify you. You said in your word, Matthew 6:33, "*But seek ye first the kingdom of God, and his righteousness; and all these things shall be added unto you.*" I pray that you will send people my way to assist with this task, and that I discern between those who are of you and not of you. I pray against any demonic forces that may try to get me off course through fear, discouragement, or procrastination. I thank you God for what you've done and what you're going to do in my life. In Jesus name, Amen."

Part 2

To Pursue

Your Purpose

8

Pursuing Your Purpose

I knew I was passionate about people who were raised without love and felt abandoned, those who searched for love and made mistakes in the process, and those who felt unworthy. These people were just like me; I had experienced those feelings as well. God often uses our experiences to lead us to our purpose.

I first thought my passion was to help others manage their finances. In life I have found that whatever moves you is what you are drawn to, and that's what you should focus on. What you would do without receiving payment is almost certainly what you're passionate about.

I prayed to God and asked Him to show me my purpose. I opened myself up to what He had to say. I remember sitting in church at a singles ministry event and the question posed by the leader was, "What would you like a double portion of?" That question caused me to reevaluate my desires to get a clear picture for my future.

Along with wanting to know my purpose, I also asked God to send me a husband that would complement that purpose. Soon after, God started revealing more of my purpose to me and opening doors for what I was sent to earth to do. I founded VAF Inspires, a company birthed to motivate women to pursue their purpose.

Years ago, I was in the market for some uplifting apparel. I searched for tee shirts with positive messages. I found several negative quotes, but didn't see many uplifting ones. It was then that I thought about starting my own tee shirt line. It wasn't until years later that I created VAF Apparel: Inspirational Rhinestone products. VAF Apparel is under the umbrella of VAF Inspires. I am doing well with my company and God is getting the glory.

You may want to start a business of your own. If so let me be the first to tell you, it is a process. What you think you want may be totally different from what the Most High wants, and that is why we should pray constantly to find out His plan for our lives.

Now that I know my purpose, I remain focused on living it. I have also ventured into other avenues such as background acting. A background actor or extra is a performer in a film or television show who appears in a non-speaking, non-singing capacity. All other activities are fine, but my main focus right now is my ministry and business. Even though I have fun as a background actor, I will always keep sight of my purpose, and wait for God's leading and guidance along the way.

I quit my part-time job of seven years to concentrate on moving my business and personal ministry forward. I enjoyed that job, but I decided I had spent enough of my Saturdays promoting someone else's business and making them rich. It was time for me to promote my own business.

I also connected with like-minded people; those who already operate their own businesses. I surround myself with people who can lead me in the right direction. When I vendor at various events, I build relationships so that, even if I don't make money, I walk away with great contacts who will help me to fulfill my purpose.

Just as it takes a village to raise a child, it takes a community to reach your destiny. God sends awesome people my way, who are more than willing to share their knowledge and experience. But there are always those who chase money, and I quickly remove myself from them. We all have to be able to discern the difference between people who are meant to be in our space and people who aren't.

I've come to realize that I must constantly learn new skills and perform some tasks for myself. This is something we all should strive to do. For example, if you're a great typist, you can type some things yourself. If you're great at creating a website, you can create one for yourself. I decided to cut out the middle-person as much as possible as I simultaneously tap into my own creativity, and in the process I learned a new phrase…do it yourself.

Frustration can occur when you search for quality help to complete your mission. The challenge is to remain determined and diligent to accomplish your purpose, with or without the assistance of others.

There are many things that motivate and inspire me. For example, I'm motivated when I see the end product of something I've designed or created, such as my rhinestone tee shirts, bags and bracelets. I get excited when I do something that's outside of my comfort zone, especially when it turns out well. I'm inspired when I envision speaking to thousands of people about pursuing their purpose. One day when I was an event vendor, someone said to me, "I can see the anointing on your life and this isn't a business for you, it's your passion. I get chills just talking to you." Those words pushed me and inspired me to press forward.

Sometimes, God will allow us to be in a place where our dissatisfaction is used to propel us into our purpose. For instance, you may have a job where you dread the thought of going to work. You could experience the feeling of dread because you're operating out of the will of God. Let me be clear, I'm not saying to leave your job. I currently work a full-time job. Everyone has to seek God when making an important decision such as this. I'm in prayer and seeking God in that area myself.

Recently, I heard a powerful preacher say that if you want an arrow to go far, you have to put the right amount of tension on the arrow. God could be adding tension to your life to propel you into a marvelous future…one you never imagined could happen.

Your purpose might not always be linked to what you do best. It could be an area where you're weak in the natural and you have to depend on God for His supernatural powers to accomplish the task.

For me, I'm an excellent speaker, but not so great with technology. I had to leave my comfort zone and conquer fear. In short, I had to go for it. We can't disregard our dependency on God. After all, if I could do it all myself, then I wouldn't need God. Thank goodness I can't because I do need Him, and so do you.

There has to be room for God and His control over your life. You can be an excellent seamstress, gifted to make costumes for your grandchildren's play or an excellent cook, gifted to love on your family and friends through food. Just because you love it, doesn't mean it's your purpose. It can be confusing. He'll expand a gift that's already inside of you.

Sometimes it's hard to differentiate between your purpose and your gift, which is why we need God. There are business owners who are successful and their businesses are thriving, yet, they may not be walking in their purpose. I'd rather live in my purpose and be in the middle class than go outside of my purpose and be rich. Being rich in God is more important.

9

Push

To push past your emotional hurts is to use the negative experience that hurt you and turn it into a positive experience for the very purpose of moving onward in your life. It is the process of intentionally promoting your own healing. You must dig deep inside of you to discover the issues that block your progress to pursuing your purpose. No one can bring healing to the unknown, the hidden hurts.

To accomplish this, search through your past and write down each incident that you can remember that negatively impacted your life. Truthfully acknowledge your feelings about each one. If this is too hard and painful, it may be wise to seek counsel from a highly trained professional; one who will gently walk you through the entire healing process. You can also study your issues by researching online, reading books or attending seminars.

For me, the attention-deficit started when I was abandoned by my father and rejected by my mother. The lack of love and attention caused me to develop unrealistic expectations in my relationships with men. I learned that my love language is attention, which is okay, but I have to know when my need for attention is healthy or unhealthy.

Forgiveness plays an important role in our healing. Yes, we may forgive, but we don't forget. To forgive is to excuse another for an offense, real or perceived. To forgive is also to let go of the anger and release the perpetrator from punishment. I had to forgive myself, just as you must forgive yourself for things you have done wrong. Sometimes you might want someone to acknowledge the pain they have caused you or to apologize for what took place. If you get the response you desire from them, great. If you don't, pray to God for strength to move on anyway.

Forgiveness is not only about the person you forgive, but it is also a gift you give to yourself; it blesses going out and coming in. Ephesians 4:32 says, *"Be kind and compassionate to one another, forgiving each other, just as Christ forgave you."* If the person is no longer around, then you might want to write a letter, seal it and either keep it or destroy it as you destroy the memories. Let them, as well as yourself, off the hook.

If you choose not to forgive, you will destroy your body. Anger, stress, and blame can show up in so many ways when it comes to your health and peace of mind. Nelson Mandela said, "Resentment is like drinking poison and hoping it will kill your enemies." Purge yourself of the poison of resentment so you can live again.

For years, I allowed my childhood pain to affect how I thought, acted, spoke and felt. After my healing process, I finally realized that the pain was part of my purpose. I can now be compassionate to others because of the pain I experienced. That specific pain was from the past...it's not welcome in my present nor my future. I changed my perspective and removed the *victim* mentality I had developed and replaced it with a *victorious* mentality. I'm no longer fragile, but fearless. I'm not abused, but awesome!

After I realized that hurting people, *hurt* people, I reasoned that maybe my parents did the best they knew how. Maybe my exes didn't know how to love, or even if they did, I couldn't recognize it. If I had known how to love maybe I wouldn't have sabotaged it. Regardless of my bad experiences with love, I am determined to keep my heart open to the people God will send my way.

While at my new church, I've had amazing experiences and revelations. Two situations stand out in particular. One Sunday, after church service, I sat in the front row uncontrollably crying. No matter how hard I tried, I could not hold back the tears as they flowed down my face. The pastor preached about a woman in the Bible who had a not-so-

Christian-like past. A woman came over to me and asked if she could console me. I told her that I was okay; trying to remain in control of the situation, nevertheless she hugged me. If you're a crybaby like me, you know when someone hugs you, it's all over.

Although she was a stranger to me in the natural realm, she became a stand-in mother in the spiritual realm. She held me like a doting mother holds her child. The last time I was held like that was when I was a little girl wrapped in my grandmother's arms. I have no memories of my mother holding me like that. God knew just what I needed and when I needed it. I was overwhelmed. We sat there, and I sobbed on her shoulders for over two hours.

Afterwards, I had an all-white event to attend. I thought I would be late, but as fate would have it, the function had not begun. When I walked in, my tears were welling up. That was a much needed cleansing experience. Some things in me needed to be released. It was not a coincidence that I wore a white dress that day and attended an all-white affair. The feeling I felt that day was worth more than money. If I could have captured and bottled it, I would have so that whenever I felt lonely or sad, I could grab it from the shelf and all would be right with the world.

My second experience was with a man. I was on my knees praying during worship time, and when I looked over, I saw a man on his knees praying as well. He asked me if I wanted him to pray for me. He prayed, and with his cane, he got back into his seat. I was so amazed that he took the time to pray for me; a stranger in the natural realm, yet a surrogate father in the spiritual realm. When God says He'll be a mother to the motherless and a father to the fatherless, He meant it.

I've found God's love through many ways. How else would God love on you unless he does it through other people? Sometimes, we get so caught up in who we want to love us, whether family or the opposite sex, that we neglect those who God sent to love us. It's not about having the same blood line, we have the same DNA when it comes down to it…the DNA of Christ. It's about His love for us, and how we receive and give it. As children of God, we should love the same way that He loves us.

Occasionally, I'm alone on holidays. Other times, God places it on someone's heart to invite me to their house. For instance, years ago I met an elderly couple in the Bahamas. We later found out that we were from the same part of town and only lived 20 minutes from each other. We have since shared holidays and birthdays. I have spiritual mothers and stand-in fathers who pour into my life, which is nothing short of a miracle. I was in Jamaica one year, and I was nervous because I hadn't ridden a horse since I was five. As I approached the horse, he rubbed his head on my chest as to say, "Don't worry, you're safe with me." I have so many stories where God sent those I needed to have in my life and removed those who should not have been there. Those experiences taught me a new love, God's love. I was more than willing to transfer that love to my new friend, the horse, so we would both take care of each other during our ride. You can never share too much of God's love, even with animals!

I also realized that you can choose your friends, but you can't choose your family. I've tried to do my part in the healing of my family, but as my counselor said, "You can't make someone get healed or be involved in your life." I keep the door open for reconciliation. I often pray for my family, and I'm allowing God to reveal how a family should unite in love.

My negative experiences are probably what pushed me into focusing on my goals, career, business, and education. I put my attention on the future and positive things like serving and helping others. When you take the focus off yourself, your situation does not seem all that bad.

I've moved forward from my hurt by realizing that my past doesn't define me. I'm worth loving, and I have something to offer to this world. My uncle often tells me that I can't change the world, but I'm doing just that, one day at a time, one smile at a time, one prayer at a time and one chapter in my book at a time. I try to live up to the saying that goes, "Be the change you want to see in the world."

To keep myself in a good frame of mind, I think and speak positive words into my life. I strive to enjoy life. I do the things that I couldn't do when I was growing up, especially things that no one did for or with me. I travel, attend social functions, and treat myself to massages. I don't wait for Mr. Right to come along and shower me with gifts. If I want something or want to do something, I work to get it done. If I don't love me or can't stand my own company, who will? I focus on what I do have, not on what I don't have.

10

What Drives You?

G od has already placed our purpose in us. Then He gives us the desire and determination to walk it out for ourselves. No one else can define your purpose for you. It is only from the Lord. Trying to find yourself any other way will cause you to be driven by someone else's reason for being on this earth. Trust me, there is no fulfillment, satisfaction or joy on that route.

You are an important member of the body of followers of the Most High. He has a plan for our lives that was determined from the very beginning. In order for His will to be accomplished in you and through you, you must have a willing spirit to follow

His lead as you seek to find your function in this world. If you don't already know your purpose, it is time to put in the work of finding your purpose.

What drives you? This can be a hard question to answer if you don't know who you are, your dislikes and likes, what really ticks you off to the point where your head will explode or what stirs you to tears.

Habakkuk 2:2-3 says, *"Then the Lord replied: Write down the revelation and make it plain on tablets so that a herald may run with it. For the revelation awaits an appointed time; it speaks of the end and will not prove false. Though it linger, wait for it; it will certainly come and will not delay."* Find a quiet place with no distractions, let go of any worries and thoughts of what you think you need to do.

Get a blank sheet of paper. To help you in this process, write down your responses to the following questions and write down everything that comes to mind. When you are done, you should have at least an inkling of your passion, and once you discover it, you will be directed to your purpose. A word of caution, don't ignore or shrug off that very thing that frightens you. Be true to yourself by frankly answering the questions.

Discovering My Purpose

1. What do you care most about?

2. What do you hate to see others do?

3. What are you good at?

4. What has God shown you that you should be doing, but put off because you don't think you *can* do it?

5. If you knew you had a short period remaining on this earth, what goal would you want to accomplish?

6. What's on your bucket list (things you want to do before you kick-the-bucket), and how can those things be used to help others?

7. Is there a significant life event(s) that disturbed you so much so that you don't want anyone else to experience it?

8. If you were to dream big, what goal do you have that you think you might not be able to accomplish?

9. What legacy do you want to leave behind for your family or for the world?

10. What do your friends know you to be most enthusiastic about?

11. What qualities do you most admire about yourself?

12. List three words that define you.

13. How would you change your community, current environment, or the world around you for the better?

14. In your childhood dreams, what was the only thing you wanted to do when you grew up?

15. What group of people, such as teenage mothers, homeless, elderly, etc. would you like to influence?

Of the 15 responses, what are the top three that most ignite your internal joy? What is it that you cannot give up on? If you had all the money in the world available to you, which one would you choose to make your life-long goal? Well, at this point, if you truthfully responded to all the questions, you should know where you are headed. Did you have that *aha* moment; the realization of that thing that inspires you most, even if it's been dormant for years? Maybe it's a book that's been sitting on the shelf or in your heart and mind...unfinished.

If you still cannot seem to figure it out, it's time to bow down and ask the Manufacturer.

11

Ask the Manufacturer

God is the manufacturer and He created us with a purpose. When we walk outside of God's purpose for our lives, we desire to please ourselves and not Him. He doesn't force anyone to walk in their purpose, but we may halt or delay God's promises when we're outside of His will. When we are faithful and commit our will to His, He'll bring our purpose to light and bring it to pass.

A few ways to discover your purpose is through communion with God, either through church services, prayer or meditation, church fellowship, or through the Holy Spirit. After we seek God, it's the Holy Spirit's job to reveal God's plan for our lives. After all, God is the manufacturer and He created us, knows us, and guides us every step of the way.

We struggle with our plans, but when we align our lives with God, His grace is sufficient. It is sometimes difficult to line up with God's plan for us because it's a struggle against our flesh, and we don't want to do the *inside* work that it takes to be ready to walk in His purpose. God has to clean up the inside beforehand, if not, we will mess it up.

If I didn't know that God had plans for this book, I would have given up a long time ago. At times, I was not in the mood to dig deep, write and re-write chapters, read and re-read chapters or take the time to sit still long enough to perfect my plan. We have to submit to God's plan for our lives in order to live life to the fullest. If you don't want to fully live, but merely survive, keep doing things your way. You will not receive the greatest blessings of a purpose-filled life, and you will die with untapped potential locked safely away in your casket.

I recently attended an event where a fellow author had a club for authors. She told me that three of her members passed away and didn't finish their books. I will be attending an event this spring. The mother didn't live long enough to see the collaboration with her daughter come to pass. These stories send chills down my spine. However, if you want the very best life has to offer, even if it means discomfort then victory, struggle, pain and disappointment until victory is won again, then try Jesus.

God is only obligated to bless and provide for His plans. If He blesses our plans, that's just His grace. He's a giving Father. So many times we make our own plans and then hope God will bless them after the fact. Proverbs 19:21 says, "*Many are the plans in a person's heart, but it is the Lord's purpose that prevails.*" When we look at *our* results, there is usually little or no progress, even when we do big things. No matter how hard we try, no matter how much money we make, no matter how much we plan or organize, we end up in the same place year after year, wondering what went wrong.

Throughout the Bible, God worked supernaturally through people to bring His plans to pass. He's the One that calls us. He's the One with the master plan. Our job is to find out what God wants us to do and then organize our lives accordingly. As long as we're headed in the wrong direction, life will be much harder because our life is out of order.

Asking the manufacturer means to seek God for the purpose in which he created you. Seek Him through prayer, scripture or counsel from others. Even if you're not a prayer warrior, just begin where you are. Prayer is communication with your Father. You don't need intelligent words, just be sincere. God knows what's in your heart, even before a word comes out of your mouth.

When discussing your purpose with others, you should seek godly and wise counsel. If what they say lines up with your passion, internal convictions, gifting's and what God has already revealed, take it into consideration.

God might not reveal your purpose in an organized fashion. He might give you pieces, a little at a time. If you're anything like me, a planner, control freak and impatient, you want to know everything at once...where He's taking you or how and when you'll get there.

You might constantly ask, "Are we there yet?" Years ago, I saw bits of my purpose, and now it's just unfolding. It's a good idea to journal when you get a revelation through sermons, prayers, songs, or other avenues. Then, you can go back to see the journey that God is taking you on, and keep a record of what He is telling you to do. This will also give you encouragement when doubt sets in and help you not to become impatient when it seems like it's taking too long.

Don't be afraid when seeking God's will for your life. Trust His plan. Proverbs 18:16 says, *"A gift opens the way and ushers the giver into the presence of the great."* In other words, God will make room for your gift. He's already given you what you need to succeed. You just have to follow through on His instructions. Even if you don't immediately discover

God's purpose or if the purpose you discovered is not clear to you, God *will* reveal it to you.

Don't procrastinate. The old saying is still true; when you take one step, God will take two. Your purpose is not just for your joy, but to accomplish something in the earth and make a difference in the life of His people. If your purpose only benefits you, you should revisit the manufacturer. One thing's consistent about God, His blessings are for His will. It's not about you.

Before you begin prayer, reflect on these scriptures for guidance:

And without faith it is impossible to please God, because anyone who comes to him must believe that he exists and that he rewards those who earnestly seek him. **Hebrews 11:6**

Then you will call on me and come and pray to me, and I'll listen to you. **Jeremiah 29:12**

Ask and it will be given to you; seek and you will find; knock and the door will be opened to you.

Matthew 7:7

And we know that in all things, God works for the good of those who love him, who have been called according to his purpose. **Romans 8:28**

12

The Pursuit

S o, you've discovered your purpose. Are you sure that it is God's plan for you? Is it a plan that is in His will? Did you come up with an idea, and now *hope* that God aligns Himself with *your* desire? Before you pursue any dream, be sure that it is what He wants you to do, then move forward…according to His plan and purpose. Listen to His directions and do what He reveals.

Now that you know or have a general idea what passion you should pursue, there are many things you should do to get started. This chapter will provide you with concrete steps to take.

Are you ready? Purpose in your heart that truth through the Holy Spirit will guide you at this moment. Excited? Let's go.

Whatever you do from here on out, will impact your life's purpose in a positive or negative way. Whatever financial, relational, spiritual, and personal decisions you make now, will play a part in fulfilling your destiny.

Understand fully what you are getting into. Know the reason why you are pursuing your dream and who will benefit from it. What is the strength of your determination to get it done? What is the exact mission you plan to accomplish? Will you quit when the going gets tough?

Having a great idea and a dream is the easy part. However, making the idea or the dream a reality can be challenging. Determine within yourself right now that you will finish, no matter how long it takes, and no matter what life brings your way, knowing in your spirit the words found in Philippians 1:6 that, "*He which has begun a good work in you will continue to perfect it until Christ returns.*"

Will you start a business? Will you mentor young people? Will you start a new ministry catering to a specific group of people? Will you teach? Does your idea have great potential? The goal in this chapter is for you to get a solid understanding of what you are getting into, and the personal impacts your choices will have on you and your family, such as money, time, energy, and other resources. To find out, you will have to invest hours in yourself by conducting the necessary research. You will need to know if you have something that is marketable, that others will support, and if it will help the group you intend to impact.

While researching, find out if there are others already doing what you want to do. Are they competitors? If so, determine the *edge* you will have over them, and use it to your advantage. Are there organizations that you can team with or join, and still be able to pursue your purpose? If so, contact them with a solid business plan and to see where you might fit in.

Learn as much as you can about the aspects of your purpose. Take a few classes, search the internet or spend time at the library researching the type of work you want to do. Study others that have already done what you're endeavoring to do and find out how they did it, including mistakes, pitfalls, and even success stories. Get a mentor to teach you the ins and outs of your purpose. Trade organizations related to your purpose is another resource. Tap into them.

Freaked out? If so, you may need to retool or rework your idea into something more manageable. If your dream is lofty, consider breaking it down into bite-sized stages…one portion at a time. If you need help, enlist others that are willing to jump on board with you. No matter what, don't give up.

After studying, then you have to map out the direction you will take. Consider putting together a document like a business or marketing plan and outline *everything*…every aspect and detail. There are plenty of resources to get you started, such as the internet, library or pay a professional to write a business or marketing plan for you.

After you've selected the identifier, then it's time to get your logo and marketing materials so that you can tell the world who you are and how you can be of service to them. If you are not graphically or artistically inclined, hire a professional to make your materials or enlist the help of a talented friend or associate. The worst thing you can do is have a great idea, plan and the money, but show the world cheap, unprofessional marketing materials. A website is an excellent tool to draw others to you so they can learn more about your venture. We live in a time where social media is vast and far reaching. Consider tapping into all avenues to market yourself and your purpose.

Networking is one strategic tool for success. It is the process of reaching out to people who can steer, teach, and direct you to others best suited to assist in your endeavor. Create a pitch that essentially sums up what you will do, something that will take one to two minutes. Then, target a few people to share your dream with. You can start small by letting those in your circle know what you are doing. Then move up to seeking those outside of your family, friends, and acquaintances. Start by attending events in your area or calling organizations and professionals that may correlate to your endeavor.

Social media can be used for networking purposes too. The more people that you are connected with, the more will know about you and your dream. Enlist others to help you or solicit their advice. Networking can be seen as selfish, but when your purpose is one to benefit others, it then becomes selfless.

Now, we all know that our plans don't always work out the way we want. What will you do if your initial plan doesn't work out? Well, you must be open to what the Most High has next for you. There are *always* options. Seek Him once again to find out. It may be in the same field, but not in the way that you envisioned it. Take the necessary time you need to figure out where you are to go and what you are to do. Those things and people that may hinder you in reaching your goals must be removed from your life. Identify them so that you will know where *not* to focus your energy.

13

Purpose Destroyers

God gave you your purpose and it's up to you to fulfill it. When we are called by God to do something, He wants us to trust Him enough to do it. Out of sheer obedience, we are to move. He doesn't arbitrarily give out His purpose. He knows what He is doing, and has already equipped us to flow in our purpose.

Does your purpose seem too large, with too many moving parts? If so, do you believe it would never work? So what! Who is God to you? If you believe in Him for the small things, and know He has come through for you, why not trust Him with the big things? Expect Him to work out the details.

There are people and things in our lives that are purpose-destroyers and goal-killers. We are the ones who restrict what God wants us to do. How? We do this by allowing purpose-destroyers and goal-killers to get in our way.

Here I will provide a few things that can get in your way…it's up to you to push past them, ignore them or completely walk away so that your purpose will prevail.

Have any of these excuses crossed your mind? Or, are you actually allowing them to keep you from pursuing your purpose?

I'd love to pursue my dream, but…

- I'm not an expert.
- I'm too young or too old.
- People might tell me to get a real job.
- It's tough in this current economic climate.
- People won't support my dream.
- I might fail.
- I don't have time.

- I don't like people.
- It's too risky.
- I'm waiting for inspiration.
- I probably can't beat the competition.
- I don't know where to start.

Or you might say…

- "I'm planning to do it."
- "I'm thinking about it."
- "I'll possibly do it."
- "I'll do it one day."
- "Maybe I'll do it soon."
- "I'll start in the new year."

If you've used any of these excuses and you haven't moved forward, then you can be your own worst enemy. You could be your own purpose-destroyer or goal-killer. We know what we should be doing, but we sometimes *consent* to self-doubt, procrastination, fear, lack of understanding, failure to prepare, poor habits, lack of enthusiasm, insecurity, unwillingness to move outside of our comfort zone, busyness with life, and reluctances to put in the hard work. Will you allow any of these to become your stumbling blocks?

Yesterday's pain and despair may not be gone, but they can be used as stepping stones into your future. If you keep looking behind you, you can't see what's in front of you. God can multitask. He can process pain and hurt out of your life while simultaneously filling your heart with joy and gladness. The unpleasant memories that we continue to rehash in our minds keeps us stuck. Unfortunately, we allow our past...hurtful events, mistakes, and failures to keep us from even getting to the starting gate. Give them over to Christ. We cannot run a race toward the end goal, our purpose, if we refuse to push past our thoughts.

When the negative recollections arise, instead of mulling over it, and feeling the emotions that come with it, we must re-train our minds to think on Philippians 4:8, *"Finally, brothers and sisters, whatever is true, whatever is noble, whatever is right, whatever is pure, whatever is lovely, whatever is admirable – if anything is excellent or praiseworthy – think about such things."*

We must think on those great things that the Most High is doing in our lives to move us in the direction of our purpose. We must discern our thoughts and line them up with scripture. Kill the falsehoods in your mind. You are worthy because God said so. He created you to walk in your purpose. You have the tools, you just have to pull them out from under the weight of your past. Leave the baggage behind you, and don't allow your purpose to be destroyed because you refuse to let go and let God. Be obedient! You are not your past.

There will be naysayers, those whose purpose is to dissuade you from accomplishing your goals. First, be careful who you share your dreams with. Not everyone will be ready to support you. They may have their own issues, but that is not to be your concern. They may be speaking from their own fears. They may care deeply about you, but not believe enough in you and the God you serve to think that you could possibly do what you set out to do.

Some naysayers may have to relinquish control or fear losing a part of you once you push past the pain to pursue your purpose. They may have legitimate concerns, but you have to remind them that it's not about them, but more about your obedience and walking in your predestined purpose. Some folks just don't deserve to watch or be a part of your journey to success. You will not have time to reassure them at every step. Move them out of your life.

Connect with those who will encourage you along the ride; those who will empower, inspire, support and even facilitate the development of your purpose. These are the ones to share your dreams with, allow to mentor you, and even be a part of the process.

The only way to overcome purpose-destroyers is to decide if you *want* to reach your goal. If so, then do it. Gather up the strength, and God will provide a way. You be the planter, and God will make your plan grow. As with biblical promises, God always asks us to do something first. What are you willing to do to succeed?

Your Personal Checklist

☐ Trust Him

☐ Listen and follow His lead

☐ Research, study and study some more

☐ Prepare

☐ Create a plan

☐ Contact assistance

☐ Pursue your purpose

☐ Stick with it, even when times are tough

Once you've done the initial work, remember:

- The pain from your past can't prevent you from pursuing your purpose if you stay focused.
- People will say, feel or think negatively but you can think positively and purposefully.

- Procrastination is from the enemy. Determine within yourself to run until you finish.
- Minor setbacks can be blessings in disguise.
- What you don't know only matters if you let it.
- Stay focused.
- Busyness is often the opposite of productivity.
- Organize your day so that you're doing one thing every day that leads to your purpose; even a small step puts you one step closer.
- Pursue! Pursue! Pursue! Go after your dreams as though your life depended on it...because it does.
- You are good enough. Believe in yourself and the God who created you.

The teacher spirit in me can't let you get away without any homework. Answer the following questions, and start pursuing your purpose today!

What is my purpose?

_____

_____

_____

_____

What action can I take today to pursue my purpose?

_____

_____

_____

_____

What do I have to push through to pursue my purpose?

_____

_____

_____

_____

Who can help me pursue my purpose?

_____

_____

_____

_____

Who can I share this book with to help them pursue their purpose?

_____

_____

_____

_____

Biography

Vanessa A. Fleeton is a woman of purpose, first-time author, motivational speaker and entrepreneur. As President of VAF Inspires, Vanessa motivates women and men of all ages and cultures to push through the obstacles of life and pursue their God-given purpose. She also created VAF Apparel, a product line that spreads inspiration through phrases embellished in rhinestones.

Her purpose manifested from the pain she experienced in early childhood. Born to a teenage mother and absentee father she struggled with where she belonged. As a result of her being freed by God from her tumultuous childhood and young adult lifestyle, she now has a heart to serve those with low self-esteem, abandonment issues and the shame of past mistakes.

Ms. Fleeton spoke at some of America's top organizations, churches, schools and non-profit organizations. As a Radio One, Inc. employee,

Vanessa was a radio personality, board operator and promotions assistant. She was also an online radio show host.

She earned a Bachelor's of Science degree in Communications from Bowie State University, an Associate of Arts degree in Business Management from Prince George's Community College, and an instructor/facilitator certificate from Langevin Training Institute.

Spending 13 years as a member of the Soul Factory in Forestville, MD until her spiritual journey led her to join Zion Church in Landover, MD, she lives to serve Christ.

Vanessa was born in Washington, DC, but was raised in Maryland where she currently resides.

To order additional copies of the book
and/or other products by this author, visit
www.vanessafleeton.com.

To schedule Ms. Fleeton to speak at your next
event, please follow speaking engagement
procedures at www.vanessafleeton.com.

Follow her on Facebook @Vanessa.Fleeton or on
Twitter @VanessaFleeton.

If this book touches your life in anyway, please
share your testimony via e-mail at
vfleeton@verizon.net.

41920689R00078

Made in the USA
Middletown, DE
27 March 2017